Hating You Is Easier Than Loving Myself

Swara Vishant Naik

India | USA | UK

Copyright © Swara Vishant Naik
All Rights Reserved.

This book has been self-published with all reasonable efforts taken to make the material error-free by the author. No part of this book shall be used, reproduced in any manner whatsoever without written permission from the author, except in the case of brief quotations embodied in critical articles and reviews.

The Author of this book is solely responsible and liable for its content including but not limited to the views, representations, descriptions, statements, information, opinions, and references ["Content"]. The Content of this book shall not constitute or be construed or deemed to reflect the opinion or expression of the Publisher or Editor. Neither the Publisher nor Editor endorse or approve the Content of this book or guarantee the reliability, accuracy, or completeness of the Content published herein and do not make any representations or warranties of any kind, express or implied, including but not limited to the implied warranties of merchantability, fitness for a particular purpose.

The Publisher and Editor shall not be liable whatsoever...

Made with ❤ on the BookLeaf Publishing Platform
www.bookleafpub.in
www.bookleafpub.com

Dedication

For those wounded by the ones they loved.
For those who carry their trauma in silence.
This is for you.
Let its wrath consume you.

Preface

I wrote these poems during some of the lowest points in my life, when I was hurting so deeply that nothing seemed to make me feel better. Everyone and everything around me told me to heal, to channel my pain toward forgiveness and recovery. But that felt impossible. It was like being asked to skip a step in my own growth, because how could I move on without first feeling the full weight of what was happening to me?

It didn't feel possible to just "snap out of it," to stop dwelling on my emotions and simply move on. So, I did what felt right at the time. I let myself completely sink into it. I allowed myself to feel every ounce of hate, loss, hurt, and anger in their full intensity. And from those moments, these poems were born.

They may seem a little disturbing because they were written by a mind in turmoil. One that was hurting and didn't know what else to do. These poems dive into psychological tension and sensual menace. They trace my journey from fear to fascination, from self-revelation to a kind of acceptance, in their own chaotic way.

I hope they bring some sense of closure to anyone

navigating a similar storm. I hope they make you feel seen and remind you that you are not alone.

Acknowledgements

To my parents, Vishant Naik and Shami Naik, for recognizing my love for poetry and nurturing it, even when it wasn't easy.

To my husband, Saish Kapadi, for your quiet strength, steady reassurance, and unwavering love.

To my daughter, Dhvani Kapadi, your birth gave me the courage to stop hiding my poems. I want you to always speak your truth, no matter how unsettling it may seem to the world.

To the Poets of Bangalore community, thank you for providing a space free of judgment, where I could share my work openly. Your support gave me the confidence to take this leap.

And finally, to BookLeaf Publishing, for offering debut poets like me a platform to share our voices with the world. Thank you for believing in me.

1. Guilty

She is guilty

Of being less like a lady,
Of being outspoken,
Of being an inconvenience to society,
Of being the kind who brings dishonour,
Of being the girl who sits with her legs wide open.

She is guilty of liking a boy,
Who plays with women like toys.
She is guilty of still wanting him,
Guilty of liking and flaunting him
Mistaken as asking for it.
Guilty of being part of a society
Where having such urges puts you
In a category of normalised assault.
"Because whores don't get raped."

She is guilty of kissing a boy
Raised in misogyny,
Where one kiss gave him the permit
To slide down a finger and much more.
She kept resisting, but he kept wanting more.
And when she finally pushed back with all her strength,

He walked out unsatisfied and labelled her "complicated."

She is guilty of being rough.
Men who did the same to other girls
They got high-fived for being studs,
While she got compartmentalised as a slut.
She is guilty of being loose.
Here, her kind is available for abuse.
She has now grown cynical of flirtation,
Afraid to trust, afraid to love.
She dates the filth she thinks she deserves,
And has grown to believe it's a privilege
That men fancy her.

She has heard those words far too often,
In a similar pattern,
By different men:
"With so much booze by the pool, I would have ended up with her in my room."
"I regret that we ever dated. How can a woman be so desperate?"
Comments she plays in her head on loop
A cycle she hopes to break one day.

She is guilty of choosing them,
Guilty of loving men
Who pulled her into their embrace,

Hoping to forget the one who got away.
After one night, they rolled away.
They lit up a cigarette
And smoked her away.

She is guilty of her hesitation,
Her inability to say no back then.
She didn't know that was an option.
She knew it felt wrong,
But didn't know she could fight back.
She knew it felt ugly,
But couldn't name it abuse back then.
She is guilty of numbing her pain.
She is guilty of silence.
She was afraid he might leave,
So she let him do it all over again.

She kept bleeding for love,
Because he just couldn't let her go.
She is guilty of not running
When she was slapped, bruised, and choked
Because she was taught that men are naive.
Taught to love them with their demons.
Taught not to scream,
Because it's crucial to protect their masculinity.
Crucial for their sanity.
She couldn't shatter a belief system

Built over centuries.

So she was deemed guilty
The day her cord was cut from her mother,
The day she was abused by misogyny,
The day she was catcalled by patriarchy,
The day she became a woman.
She was doomed to die
As a prisoner of their mentality.

2. Outsider

Some called me an observer,
Others, a silent spectator
For peeking into their lives,
For hiding behind my books.

Some called me a snob,
Others, a prude
For being lost in a different life,
For living in worlds built by my books.

I was an outsider,
Watching teenage boys place their girls on pedestals.
But they looked through me,
Made me believe I was invisible
Because fat girls didn't deserve love.

I was an outsider,
Yet I wanted to be like you.
But I couldn't laugh at your humour,
Couldn't dance to your tunes,
Couldn't tan in your May,
Or soak in your June.

I was an outsider,

A loner in my assigned corner.
Silenced by your noise,
Watching you forge unbreakable bonds,
Make promises of true love
While I was tangled in judgments and body hair.
Beauty's definitions felt rigid at twelve.

I was an outsider,
My voice drowned
By your passive-aggressive conversations
Conversations I was too naïve to comprehend,
Conversations that picked apart my hesitations.
My hesitations became the centrepiece of your conversation.
Your blankets of whispers made me shiver.
I grew skeptical of every conversation.

I was an outsider,
Too afraid to even mutter,
Too afraid to move through those packed corridors.
I recognized those hands too well
The ones that groped amidst chaos, then vanished,
Slipping into a swamp of other hands.
Maybe I'd be safe if I stayed mute.
The last time I raised my voice against this abuse,
I was ridiculed, called an attention whore
A name that snowballed into a fear of humans,

A fear that turned into a book full of poems.

I'm sorry if I saw you.
Sorry if I stared.
Sorry if I spoke.
Sorry if I spilled a few words here and there.
I didn't know my syllables were your wealth,
That you'd twist them into your narrative
Because you, too, were battling insecurities
I couldn't begin to understand.

I'm sorry for hating you.
Sorry for wanting revenge.
I'm learning to forget.
Sorry for wishing to be one of you.
Sorry for wishing to be popular.
Sorry for existing
As your unwanted outsider.

3. Insatiable

Just one bite
of creamy, gooey cheese
for the four-year-old
who is never hungry.
She isn't chubby,
She isn't adored by many.
But the sparks in her eyes reveal possibilities
of a future so bright,
It might burn her alive.

Just one bite
of something sweet
chocolates and caramel pudding.
This metamorphosis they call puberty
makes her want to stuff her face,
because she's always hungry.
Now they grab food out of her hand.
"Watch your weight," they say.
"Maintain the beauty of items to be sold."
"Marriage doesn't come with a returns policy."
Words like these
spoken so casually
from those meant to nurture
tear her self-worth slowly.

Just one bite
of protein bars and broccoli.
She wishes she could puncture her body,
deflate herself into something skinny.
She can't bear it anymore
those eyes gawking in disgust,
constantly counting her flabs,
until she decides to take matters into her own hands.
Losing weight,
burning all that she can,
sleeping hungry and exhausted,
hoping someone
will still want to hold her hand.

Just one bite
of anything toxic
to make it all go away.
Those same eyes
now gawk with pure lust.
She scrubs, and scrubs, and scrubs
but she cannot erase their touch.
They justify it by saying,
"Boys like your tiny waist and pretty face."
But God forbid
that body comes with opinions.
God forbid if she says,

"This is not okay.
Your advice,
your comments,
your jokes and justice,
turn into eating disorders,
make body dysmorphia my reality,
leave me insatiable.
I'm still that same fat girl,
now trapped in a skinny body."

4. Three Little Birds

Three little birds
I locked in a cage.
Three little birds that flew away
They flung the door open
And shattered all my chains.

The first to escape
Was painfully naive,
Even gullible, one might say.
Because of him, it started
A silly game of flames.
I wonder if it was even love,
Or why it broke so easily.
Now it all seems foolish.
The first bird flew away when I was fourteen.

The second was tougher.
His actions- brutal, rough.
He didn't just escape;
He flew right through me,
Armoured in deceit.
He shredded my love into pieces,
Pecked at the tender parts of my heart.
He made me bleed.

It took me years to heal.
I was nineteen when I lost him.

After that, I grew cautious.
I forged a few more locks,
Switched the chains to titanium,
Plated the cage with gold
An incentive, a manipulation.
There would be no escape from this one,
I promised myself.
I won't let the third bird go.
I refuse to live with an empty soul.

My last bird will stay forever
If I don't play with him,
If I don't touch him,
If I don't let anyone near him.
We'll survive in this solitude
Till I turn twenty-two.

But that's when my charmer came.
His genuine moves devoured
The bird I had trained.
He wasn't my usual type
Not like the ones I used to crush on,
Not like those with chiselled jawlines.
Yet he spun sweet words like candy floss,

Then hardened them with lust,
And cracked open my cage.

He lured out my little birdie
With relatable imperfections
And tales of compatibility.
He walked in without warning
And quietly wrecked my beliefs.
Innocence, sanity, comfort
All three birds flew away, one by one.

My cage is now empty,
But its shimmer still invites suitors.
Such is the power of infatuation.
After I lost the dream of building my forever,
I began to see a different world
All the possibilities I once ignored
While obsessing over my precious birds.
After they flew away,
I examined the wings they left behind.
Now I can fly too
With my empty cages
And a heart full of dreams.

5. Morning Routine

Things changed.
Some were added,
Some were subtracted.

Like any other Monday, I woke up,
Got dressed,
Had my coffee,
And headed to college.

I woke up
but I hadn't slept at all.
I haven't been sleeping for a while.
Even after intoxication,
Even after exhaustion,
Sleep feels unattainable.
Peace, unapproachable.

I had my coffee,
but even the creamer tastes bitter.
My appetite has disappeared;
I can't taste sugar anymore.
Is this the price I pay
for the darkness I desire?

I dressed up,
but I don't feel pretty anymore.
No matter how much I contour,
When I look into the mirror,
I don't recognize her anymore.

I headed to college.
I flinch at every moment
that passes in silence.
I let loud music assist me now
because silence is too painful.
It makes me anxious;
it makes me remember
what I have lost,
what I once had,
what I will never be able to give.
It makes me forget
my reasons to live.

6. I see

Our eyes spoke
More than our lips ever did.
Before we began,
And after we ended things.
They noticed you
Even when I wasn't searching.

Not because you were unique,
Nor because they sought someone ordinary
Yet they were stuck on you.

I still don't know why,
But I didn't seem to mind.
You felt like you were worth it, for a while.

I still miss those days
When mystery lingered,
When you placed me on a pedestal.

I admit, I was selfish too.
I loved being the only one
In your world.

An unforgettable walk began with,

"Our compatibility is uncanny,"
And climbed the hilltop of
"You belong to me."

Only for you to push me off that cliff.
I shattered.
I'm still breaking.

Eyes are stupid
They gawk at the worst times.

Right after closure slipped away,
I saw you in a mirror.
I saw you replace me with her.

Those same eyes,
That same smile,
That same hope in your heart.

So tell me
Do you touch her
The way you once caressed me?

I can see your eyes searching for her,
The way they once looked out for me.

Tell me

Do you say it to her too,
Those words you once whispered to me?

I try to let the similarities console me,
But I'm confused by our sameness.

This substitute you found so easily
It feels more like science
And less like love.

She cannot be me.
She just cannot be me.

But I see
You're sculpting an image of me in her.
Unaware, she lets you chisel.
She also believes
What I once believed.

I see the same hope in her eyes.
What if I, too, never meant anything?
What if you're still searching
For the one you lost
In her,
In me,
In everyone
And everything.

7. The Hunt

It takes more than canines
To be a predator.
So don't muzzle every fang you see.
Some also hide in sheep's clothing.

Spot the dilated pupils
When they watch the blood spill.
It takes more than those bloodstains
To be a predator.

A lust for holes in the skin,
A salivation for blood and teeth,
Hands that rip all sleeves,
Hands that smash faces into the earth,
Because only then does their manhood harden
At cries begging for mercy.

The warmth of her breath
Feels moist on their skin.
Arms choke her neck
As they watch her fight to save that pathetic life
Which is somehow worth living.

She let them into this house that she built.

So why does she scream at the sight of this beast?
How are plucked canines better than visible claws?
It's not only the weapon that makes one a monster.

Deer's horns are sharper than a wolf's growl.
And Bambi won't warn you with an echoing howl.
Yet they both cut equally deep.
Disturbed souls can make the mighty weep.

But we still let the deer in,
Because we fear red eyes more than a camouflaged smile
Smiles demonic enough to carve our hearts out.
They make a great souvenir for a killer's wall,
Each with its own story and a unique flavour.

All wolves don't pile on carcasses,
Some deer don't feast on grass.
Urges few live as love,
While others project twisted fetishes.

There is something animal about those instincts
A scratch on the back,
A choking of the neck,
Fingers hook mouths;
Unprocessed feelings come out.

Some find death appealing,

Some fixate on a heart that is still beating.
Those who wield the power of a knife
May walk the ruins of night,

Hunt for the ones
Who curse strength with weakness,
Who walks the atonement for flesh,
Who devoured wombs
To dine in candlelight before the doom.

Only then will you see
The predator in a rabbit's eyes,
In Bambi's smile,
Hear the victim in the wolf's cry.

It takes more than a name to be a predator.
It takes more than fangs to bite,
More than horns to fight,
More than words to hurt,
More than a fire to burn,
More than an instinct to hunt.

Distinguish between the wolf who is blunt,
And the bruises you count
Those left by the deer you loved.
It takes more than our narrative to be a victim.
It takes more than your perspective to hunt.

8. Lips

Wicked little things
Plump or petite,
Crusty or soft,
But always sweet
When he desires to taste it.

Loud, these things can screech
At a deafening frequency,
But they're ordered to stay shut.
Assured that nothing is wrong,
They often remain unheard of.

Abusers often turn deaf,
In the dead of night,
when their senses come alive.

Lies gush from the same
From deceitful souls,
From men who lost honour
In the arms of a whore.

A whore who once was a lady,
Before she was chewed up
And spat out by teeth

Teeth she had mistaken for bones,
Bones strong enough to lift her.

Kisses change mouths
As the honeymoon magic fades.
Fairy tales end
Before life turns mundane.

Promises shift priorities,
Whispered now to a different ear.

It is an easy carriage,
Travelling from lips to lips,
Across her body,
Mapped by sports bases.
That is what we make of a female body.

It is forbidden,
Hence desired.
Once touched,
It is marked as ordinary
As if his fingers were worthy enough
To absorb all that she holds,
And all that she could give.

Still, she is compartmentalized after use,
Or tossed out on the streets,

For another pair of brown, red, or pink lips.

They feast in the night,
And shame in the daylight.

9. Voices

Misinterpreted notions.
Unheard stories.
Everyone has an opinion
About my legacy.

My freedom
My empowerment
Feels like those lovers' kisses
Whose eyes stay open.
I feel incomplete.

Your quarantines don't scare me.
The voices locked in bodies
Keep echoing inside
Internalizing ever-changing notions,
Making me question
These evolving circumstances.

We learned to make a living
By selling handcuffs and chains.
What should I do
With this empowerment?

I am aggressive.

I am submissive.
I am growing,
Yet I remain unexpressive.

I choke in your throat.
I rule your brain.
I am the voice
Of a tongue that was cut
From a body that was burnt
Now dangling
As a showcase.

10. Castle

Some nights, I strip away my projections,
my added layers of protection
another sad attempt at deception.

I feel the urge to press myself against you
You, with a strong, cold build.
You are so thick,
even I can't penetrate in.
You exhale calmness
while harnessing my chaos within.

You are the wall I built,
in my little space
where I can barely fit a bed,
and books in my cabinet
yet somehow, I still manage to fit
insecurities, abnormalities,
bloodlust-triggering activities.

I press my body against yours.
I tremble in the cold
as your snowflakes melt into me.
I don't know how to house
these flakes amid

my flames that are always burning me internally.

I'm still trying to comprehend this duality.
I live in my stone-cold castle,
built brick by brick
from my lover's bones
and my girlfriend's blood
bound together
with the feelings that betrayed my gut.

I am not evil.
I do wish to push through,
to break through
maybe let a window open accidentally,
let a lover in
who, I know, will only see my crazies.

He will define me by those boundaries.
He believes girls like me can take it all in
be his bitch,
cry, bleed,
moan for him.

I will let you believe it.
I will ask you to choke me
choke my freedom,
choke my voice,

choke my existence.

I will let this crystal-bright beauty
merge with your skin.
I will let my snowflakes
melt into your body.

And in my embrace, you will perish.
With my poison,
you will perish.

After your memories rest six feet deep,
I will watch my walls
grow another inch
with your blood,
your bones,
your gut
that once led you to me.

11. Destructive

I wonder what it's like to hold the sun.
I've heard enough love stories
Told by your moons.

I wonder if that ball of fire
Might just warm the skin
That's been burnt inside out
By so many who twinkled like you.

Stars and their narcissistic flames
Destroy more than they ever create,
Leaving me searching for the next bright thing,
Hunting for closure
In empty promises.

What mysteries do you hold
In your tender embrace?
Will your touch thaw me
Or turn me to ashes?
Will you harden me instead,
Into a stone colder
Than those frozen bodies?

Bodies from my past.

Bodies from yours.
Bodies whose spines we pulled out,
Click by click
So they stood still
Only in our embrace.

We are both warriors
Of the same PTSD.
How long until it explodes,
And turns you against me?

How long until we both become
Just another body
A body with a beating heart
And a dead soul,
A body that stopped living
A long, damn time ago?

12. Butterfly effect

Yes, the apple didn't fall far from the tree.
It dropped into the pond nearby
into the one who helped the tree blossom,
the one who gave her those tears.

She's the one who suffered his ripples,
the ones that made his daughter fall for stones
stones that broke her spine and bones.
Yet she kept begging for more.

This raised her to dream of a love
no one should ever wish for.

She befriended familiar strangers
one who looked like him,
the one who got her addicted to pain,
the one who made her fixated on hate.

She fell for the stones,
searching for a chest hard enough,
whose beating heart felt like his bark.

These smooth stones now cuddle his daughter,
but their hard exteriors can never imitate her father.

The apple that wished to swim far away from her tree somehow got stuck in the puddle.

This generational trauma
comes around in circles.

13. Red Riding hood

She was a kleptomaniac.
She stole little things
red flags and snake skins
from every relationship she had been in.

She stitched them into a cozy little hood
for the days she had to enter the woods,
inhabited by big, bad wolves.

This wouldn't be her first visit.
The back of her neck was filled
with bite marks their kind had left in the past
a reminder of every night
she walked through the forest and survived.

She would drip blood
and disappear in plain sight,
watching the wolves roam the same path.

They smell her.
They can't have her.
Her hunt has grown immaculate.

They see the knives,

yet they can't deny the urge
to sink their fangs in one more time.
They've heard stories
of flesh that tasted so good
from a cousin who devoured
the Red Riding Hood.

While hunting for another deterrent,
she saw a furry grey hide come her way.
His whiskers glistened under sunlight.
She can't feel this way again
a hunter can't afford to fall in love with the prey.

He tiptoed in to rip the judgments
she kept wrapped
in her blanket statements.

Her wounds bled when he licked.
She tried not to flinch.
She believed there was no heart left to steal.
He didn't argue
but he didn't step back, either.

He helped her sweep
the shattered pieces of that broken heart.
When she handed him the cleaning shift,
he slipped a couple of pieces into his pocket.

They went unnoticed.

With no promises of forever,
but one paper cut at a time,
we write forbidden romance
on sharp-edged paper as a sign.

Stories like these are often told
to warn the lover in us
and the crimes they yearn for.
Stories that betray us
to give a lesson
against the next hand we might hold.

14. Autopsy

A realization. An epiphany.
What scary little things they can be.

It took me back to the same crossroads
I always run away from.
I had once shut down at a similar intersection.

I had an epiphany
about an old nightmare
molding into a dream.

I don't think I am suicidal,
but I often encounter sensations when asleep,
where I am falling off cliffs.
And I wake up weak in my knees,
sweating in panic,
just to return to a monotonous reality.

So, on a blissful afternoon I spent in a mud house,
surrounded by madmen like me,
I lay down on that naked ground.

Soon my bones absorbed the chill through my skin.
Icy thoughts walked in that open space,

collecting snowflakes escaping in the air we exhaled
comforting us misfits.

What if the next time I fall, I don't wake up from that dream?
I could just sink into the earth and not crack open.
Let it embrace me
be one with it.

Crumbled soil might make sense of the feelings
that often thrive on demolishing my sanity.
A mother's hug repairs every broken piece.

I let her spread her roots into the void
I've been filling with bad boys and pastries.
I could let her perform an autopsy,
but I'm afraid of who I'll find
living inside this shell
whose poems are so psychotic,
I don't wish to unleash
who I am hiding.

15. Snow globe

I like the leprechaun,
and I love my pot of gold too.
The warlock with a fiery heart I dream of
lives by my window
on a faraway tree, in my snow globe.

Under the dome, they stay,
as their pixie dust triggers allergies.
At the end of the rainbow,
we hunt for currencies.

The little green man ran out of wishes.
He spotted the footprints
of the shoes he mended,
played mischief on his riches.

Little mushrooms where elves once lived
my buddies ate them up,
plucked a few fairy wings
and smoked them like cannabis.

Got high off my fantasies,
they vandalized my voices.
So I built this dome

out of Xanax and morphine.

They can lick and lick,
but soon they will perish.
By the time they reach the center,
before they touch the world I cherish,
before they cut down my faraway wonder

We will skin their bodies
for those cold nights.
We will get cozy in their hide.

I live in my snow globe
that I keep by my window.
The one you meet,
in your mundane realities,
is just my shadow.

16. 6th of October

6th of October
The night stretched long.
Winter made the marks more evident
marks his fingerprints left on her neck, her face.
They became more and more alive
with every hand he raised.

After he was done with his woman,
after her eyes swallowed her tears,
she poured after midnight,
choking on her pillow every night.
She would hold herself tight,
sleeping in his bed, every night.

6th of October.
Nights stretched long.
This winter made their love more evident
when he grabbed her a shawl
and held her hand as they stepped out for a night walk.
He spoke about how she made his life better,
how he was glad they stuck together
even after all these years
countless fights and a child later.
They stared at the stars in each other's arms,

and pictured a forever together.

It looked like the same date
But it wasn't the same night
a life stretched decades apart.
I watched her break herself down
to let him build his desired wife.
From the sidelines, I always watched.
I am a mixture of their blood,
and I am still searching
for damage in every man I encounter.

17. Exceedingly regular

I am a girl
They prefer to call exceedingly regular.

I bare hands that pull a sari
Instead of a luxurious gown
For the nights filled with an intimidating crowd.

An old, wise, but familiar aura comforts me
This cloth that touched generations.
It saw their glory,
Their cupboards full of riches.
It suffered their debts,
Witnessed minds that turned rags into silk drapes.

This choice is more than vintage;
I feel royal, wrapped in my heritage.

I bare feet that refuse to step on the lane
Leading to the colourful nightlife.
I once couldn't resist its shine
Its deafening music and blinding lights.

Now it seems empty,
Shallower than a mirage,

Not sturdy enough to shatter
Built for a train of thought that has lost it way.

Here, glasses swirl liquid gold
And thin blood that stains.
Here, mouths chug it to numb heartache;
Rooms filled with blazers and sequins harness pain.

I am not your girl next door
The one who is easily doable.
Neither am I the kind
From your parents' approval.

I dwell in a twisted equilibrium.
Some call me a prude,
Others believe I am plain rude.

So let them label me, misread my spark,
In the shadows, my truth boldly thrives;

Because I am not alone.
We all have a war of perspectives to withstand
These troubled waters we must dive into now and then,
Just for the realization that
With shut eyes, this life had begun,
And with shut eyes, it will end.

18. She

We have read her in many analogies
a slice of medium-rare meat.
She is that honey so sweet;
for you, she will drip.

A tree whose flowers you pluck
and fruits you devour,
yet she continues to give.

She is your wildest dream,
a masterpiece of every art she's painted in
so fragile, she stands still only in your embrace.
She needs a protector, or she will fall from grace.

Waists judged by the swing,
lips questioned by the wine she sips
pure or dirty,
all of her is for your benefit.

But,
she is too lucid to fit in the boxes we build.
So she wishes to change the narrative;
she flows, cutting the edges,
shaping her path.

Some call her shameless,
others desire her tint.
She is living her wildest dream;
she now lives for herself
and won't cater to your every need.

She blossoms.
She is raw.
She will cook for her belly,
And not be your meal.

Women of every century
bear the bitter truths from the mother's womb
the guilt of living for herself, which isn't permitted.

She was a poem that he wrote,
but now, she writes flawlessly.

She is no longer your feature.
She won't be your past, present, or future.
Her limbs have carried your weight long enough.
Her eyes have cried your tears.
Her heart has sheltered your fears.

The day she shed you
oh, how she flew,

free of your guilt.

So call her shameless,
call her selfish,
call her a waste of a woman, for she won't bear kids.
She is more than her womb and clit,
more than a mother or a pleasure,
more than a purpose for your manhood to protect,
more than your honour,
more than your horror.

Look beyond the roles you trap her in.
She is still fighting, restlessly
to be everything
you wouldn't let her be.

19. Bon Appetit

A thousand dishes cooked
From the same protein
Some umami, some sweet,
With a sizzle to cut through her meat.

You skinned her feathers, you tweezed her fat,
To make her look more glossy,
To trigger your appetite.

You glazed her pieces with caramel;
The sugar burnt, and so did she.
That made her shiny,
Malleable and dip-worthy
Left you licking your fingertips,
Fingertips that you dipped in her truth,
Because yours tasted bitter
And hers was too sweet.

You tossed her in your spices,
Infused her with all that heat.
It made your hunger cry;
It made you crave another bite.

Identical are those who devour

And those who cook
Those who slurp her broth
To fill their empty souls.

Treachery burns your kitchen flames;
Your words are enough to lubricate.
You cook your women
Those inconvenient and unwanted.

You seep into her
The flavours that you lust for;
In your grip, she broils
At a temperature you desire.

Now with a melted soul and crispy heart
Bon appétit for your work of art.

Enough is enough.
All of you chefs have loved enough.
I have been burnt enough,
I have been broiled enough.

Now I am peeling off my soot
So I can be raw again,
So I can bleed again,
So I can live again.

I have escaped from your kitchen.
Now, no knife can touch me.
Now your words can't cut me.

So beware, my lover, my beloved
The next time you approach me
With your deceitful condiments,
You will be burnt
By the fire I now nurture,
The one you once ignited in me.

20. Confetti

Saw a distorted image in my mirror,
And I shattered it into pieces.
The mess in my room resembled confetti,
Because these broken glasses refract
A life that I had led.

Sometimes, the whole image
Is a bit too much to comprehend,
So I analyzed every bit individually.
I pulled the bin close,
To throw away a confetto or two
But I couldn't.

For they were once a part of me.
Hence, I keep my wreckage close.
With this baggage, I'm healing.

I hold no regrets.
I hold no grudges.
If my past was rotting,
Then its lessons cured my present
Only for me to blossom in the future.

21. Monster under my bed

When the sunshine creeps in,
and its light unites with my bedroom floor,
his grip fades a little
but never disappears completely.

There is a monster under my bed;
only in moonlight is he visible.
My screams don't travel
not through the door,
nor through the walls.

When he climbs to the top
and scrapes down all my layers
the ones I struggled to grow over the years
now I am naked.
Now I am exposed.
Now I am vulnerable.

All of my wounds are visible,
the ones I tried so hard to cover up with humour.
As I scream in agony,
my monster won't cover my face.
My monster wants to see me in pain
the pain the rest of the world asked me to cover up.

He wants me to relive it all over again.
His eyes draw out my terrors.
His tongue sips on my tears
as they roll down my neck.

He holds my heavy chest;
his kisses on my belly
churn out my deepest insecurities.

My monster knows my lust.
My monster can feel those feelings
that lay hidden in my gut.
My monster always lingers.

He only loves me in my sorrowful state.
My monster fears
to disclose his existence.
Under my bed, he's safe.
In my puddle of tears, he's safe.

Only in the darkness of the night
does he swim up to the surface.
Under the moonlight, we fornicate
filthy and raw, yet pure.

We die a little every single day.

But only with my monster
do I feel secure.
I feel at home.
I feel safe.
I feel sane.

He tears through sugarcoated curtains;
now my vision is clear.
Now I see
that the world isn't black or white
it's shades of blue and grey,
with very little hope and lots of pain.

Now I can see through people,
and the colours that they hide,
and the neutrality that they project.

My monster disclosed to me
the world that we live in
and the poison it injects.

22. Clay Woman

I wasn't born,
I was created
a perfection they desired.

I was sculpted,
my clay so soft.
They shaped me with morals and values
they hoped would keep me pure.

The water they used to work the clay
had a hue of narcissism,
with hints of brutal discipline
bitter words, slaps, and kicks.
A woman was shaped properly.

The colour palette was neutral,
so I wouldn't be expressive.
Fair maiden, well-dressed and skinny,
ripped jeans camouflaged under salwar kameez.

But now and then, a desire screamed
to say more,
do more,
to show more skin.

They shut me up
with words so hot.
They said this fire was necessary
to harden the pot,
to dry out the moisture,
to dry out desires,
to dry out emotions
things that could potentially crack their creation.

Their fire burned my raw sexuality,
a fire that scorched emotions that I wished to feel,
a fire that consumed my hopes and dreams
because such things,
their rigid beliefs couldn't permit.

My lips were sealed
with the trust they carved
into my melancholic brain.

A broken vase they unknowingly created.
They forgot to weigh the value
of my personality,
of what I could have been,
before I was put up for sale.

But the day my throat choked,

the day my voice broke,
my skin rippled,
and my spine shook

my eyes told the same story again:
The tale of what parents created
not the perfect woman,
but a perfect wife-to-be-wed.

23. Ghost

Water holds memory.
In every drop,
in every ripple
that's why the blood remembers
the sins this body didn't commit.

Sirens who reside
in these black waters
lust over my regrets,
and my darkest memories.
Their voices in my head
thrive on my horrid fate.

Some say my blood is poisoned
the one that runs through my veins.
Women from my ancestry devoured joy,
and that's what my body shares.
Their facts define me.

Water holds memory.
And it remembers the blood that was splashed.
The stream that fills our well
also remembers the people who stared
into its deep abyss.

The water remembers
how it pulled them close
with a promise of peace in its darkness.

Droplets that pour every monsoon
through the cracks in our roof
they are welcomed by their salty sisters,
the ones always part of her cheeks,
because her heart is filled with guilt.

Water remembers.
It ran through her unfaithful body.
Now, decades later,
it flows through the conscience of her daughters.

It remembers her past sins.
Now her blood must face the repercussions.
Now it demands atonement
for the souls she allowed to sink
into her eyes
that resemble a deep abyss.

24. Comfort Zone

I live in melancholy,
my sky is never blue.
It is pale grey most days.
It pours.

The sun doesn't shine here;
its rays pierce my eyes
when they enter my house.
I see your homes
overflowing with natural light.
Alas, I will never have that brightness
in mine.

Sweet memories fade.
Bitter truths
remain engraved in my brain.
I call them lessons.
But really,
I just love to hate.

Waves on the beach
wash away my sorrow.
Two puffs,
and my soul goes mellow.

Brightness
a belief, a happy fate
things my reality
cannot touch.
Maybe that's why
I just love to hate.

I live in this town of melancholy.
My cottage—gloomy,
my rains—my only love.

I curl up
with a blanket full of grudges,
a cup of bitter black coffee
warming a dark soul
that is always grim.

My life—always brewing,
oozing sadness,
yet somehow
soothing.

25. Black Widow

Those perfections in paintings
the ones you compare your women with
red lips, protruding tits,
skin soft as silk,
sitting on a pedestal,
naked yet graceful,
with that look that begs,
"Won't you please come and fuck me?"

An unrealistic fantasy, painted
for your hungry eyes to feast
lies that taste so sweet.
Because reality is too ugly:
the rolls on her tummy,
pimples on her cheeks,
hair in her armpits.

What nature built is too ugly,
so you believe you can repair her errors,
make her pretty.
You try to make her aesthetically pleasing.
For you, she's just a dish
waiting to be garnished.

You say women are your vices
that I am a drug,
and you, the addict.
One taste, and your mind swears
you'll be satisfied for eternity.

But here's the funny thing about vices
they leave you insatiable.
You always come back, craving more.

And you guessed it right:
she's not a drug.
She's destructive.

She built this web
its beauty, your obsession
but it wasn't made for you to admire.
This infatuation was spun
to trap her prey,
for her to devour.

This battle was designed
for her to win.

26. Dark Places

It sent a chill down my spine
As the clock struck twelve.
The haunted mansions began calling
They whispered, and started staring.

"Tiptoe, so that he won't listen."
Ghouls secure the den of Satan.
Here, leaves turn blue,
And black are their stems.

As I enter the garden of hell,
I see butterflies screech,
And roses that look bloody red.
Here, bonfires burn,
Serving s'mores so sweet
But the marshmallows are poisoned,
Bones are used as sticks.

I see vampires wield wooden stakes
To tear into the meat,
And werewolves use silverware.
While you wrap your mind
Around this deceit

Why does Lucifer look like my lover?
Why does this lingerie look so familiar
The one that Lilith wore
To wrap him around her fingers?

Has the infidelity made him forget,
Or have I gone delusional?

These mansions dripping blood
Don't scare me anymore.
I see the moon through the glass ceiling,
Though it doesn't shine like it did before.

A throne made of thorns awaits—
For me to rule them all,
To torture them,
And drink their sinful fate.

Then I realize:
I look like Lilith once I strip my lies.
She is born out of my memories;
In the corners of my mind,
These dark places are lurking—
Demons are feasting
On the remains of my sanity.

In these dark places,
I just might live happily.

27. Down the Rabbit Hole

I wear a dark velvet soul
with my pink silk dress.
I like lots and lots of cream
while everyone drinks their coffee black.

I look like a doll,
but I move like a cat.
I may look like Alice,
but I act a lot like the one who wears the hat.

Itsy-bitsy Red Queen screams,
"Off with her head!"
Hush! don't tell her.
It's this camouflage that I dread

I like the blue on Alice
more than little Cinderella,
maybe because the voices in my head
play grim tales like a cappella.

So I don't let the world know
what goes down the rabbit hole.
I put on a doll face
and hide the stories down below.

Act! How they like it.
Act! How they want you to be.
Shut down your reflexes
don't surface your crazies.

My brain might be scattered;
it mumbles like the Mad Hatter.
But I often see, around me,
everyone's going a little bonkers.

So why should I hide?
Why should I pretend?
When the world seems to go insane

I don't want to put on a show.
I won't give Adam another blow.
Lucifer tastes so much better;
Can his fire consume me whole?

With shadows as my only kin,
in the land of quirky mirth,
I'll find solace within my sin,
Because I lost my sanity in my drive to win

28. Book Cover

Little Miss Prude
she is sculpted differently
than those around her.

Little Miss Prude
she is perceived wrongly
by those who surround her.

Because the shape of her body
and the values that run within
contradict each other constantly.

Plump are her lips,
toned is the muscle beneath,
something that makes her curves exquisite.
But a taste is what she refuses to give.

She knows she deserves better
than the attention she receives.
She's more than just a pretty face;
she knows what she deserves,
and that—she'll take.

Don't be intimidated by her.

She won't act nice, but she is kind.
She just doesn't let your flaws define
her self-worth within the limits you confine.

A woman of high value,
too many layers she hides.
She can mold into anything you fantasize,
but a woman like her comes with a price.

Deceived by many,
cherished by few,
Little Miss Prude
deals with issues
wars she wages constantly with her truth.
Yet she remains hopeful,
Though she grew up with abuse.

Little Miss Prude
you are a book worth reading.
Your chapters are freaky,
they can turn people into junkies.

Excellent is your high,
the strokes between your thighs
but so are the thoughts that you spill,
so is the love in your eyes.

Little Miss Prude,
don't you dare compromise.
The world will judge
the shine of your cover every single time.

Some will crave that glitter,
some will shame it and call you bitter.
But if they don't even bother to read,
their judgments don't mean a thing.

You are more than just a book cover.
Little Miss Prude,
Your story is honest, sweet, and pure.

29. Picture Perfect

White, white canvas
Spilled shades of red.
Each stroke is a little different,
With water thicker
Than blood that once looked so red.

Father, Father,
am I just plastic?
The shape you give, I melt and mould in.
Little Miss Perfect, a prize for men to win
Do you even hear my midnight screams?

Brother, brother,
am I just a piece of meat?
When intoxicated, did it make you slip?
Your wet fingertips,
My blood on your sleeves
Like the women who moan
On your mobile screen.

Lover, lover,
was I just a toy?
To play with because your mommy broke your joy?
Sugar on your lips, and the games you deploy

My cuts and bruises are yours to enjoy.

White canvas turned blood-red.
She's miserable, but picture-perfect.
Her eyes have gone dry
Love that she shed
Leaving her a little less alive,
A little more dead.

30. Pity Pretty

Who left the faucet open?
Who let these salty drops overflow?
It's making my heart prune
a momentary relief, a soft blow.

What if I cover it with snow?
My scars are still fresh down below.
Now my skin's turned into leather,
and paint fills the lines on my skin.
Once where emotions lurked,
it's now replaced by its venomous kin.

I'll be your sin,
you'll be my sinner
with a weaponized kiss,
my addictive killer.

They say
"Do not love her.
Do not heal her.
She's turned into Lilith,
but like an angel, she glimmers."

So, if you desire my honesty,

then prove that you are worthy.
For my truth has been used
as a weapon against me.
Until then, you consume
the lies that I feed.

31. You

With a flicker in her eyes
and a charming smile,
"Love ya," she said,
as she waved goodbye.

So you wait.
You wonder.
You watch.
And then
you realize:
the words on her lips
don't match the threads in her mind.

You try to tie
knots of those loose ends,
count every penny you spent,
hold up this image
you tried so hard to pretend
never spilling truth,
never making amends.

Theories you spin.
Roles you cast her in.
Calling her a golddigger.

A tease prick.
Until you forget
what to believe.

Words lose meaning.
And with these lies,
you start living.

Sometimes
it's hard to see.
Why did it start
in the beginning?

So you dig deeper.
You cross all lines.
Hoping.
Praying.
That there is a reason
you might find.

You hope it'll all be fine.
But the steps you take
create a space
between what you claim is yours
and what I know
is mine.

32. Dear Prince Charming

Dear Prince Charming,
You don't entice me anymore.
I've seen all those white horses you rode,
In shiny armour, custom-made
To hide the demons you promised you'd slayed.
But you are still bound by their orders,
Which you must obey.

So you hope
This peasant girl can numb them for you,
But you refuse to reciprocate,
Because she's lucky enough to step foot in the castle.
How dare this lowlife demand diamonds?

Stories knit fantasies of your alluring grace
Of this man who remembers her foot size,
But not her face.
Heroically saving her that day,
With these fetishes that have come along the way.
Who cares about kingdoms, bureaucracy, and defence?
As long as you have a pretty little thing with tiny legs.

To you I say:
Please. Spare me.

Spare me your glass slippers.
Spare me your icy heels.
I won't fit into your spineless beliefs.
I have a sturdy back.
A high neck.

You asked her to let her hair down
So you could climb into her heart.
You want her innocence,
Because you lost yours to melancholy.
You'd rather climb her hair
Than set her free.
Because your entitled shoulders
Can't hold responsibility.

It's exhausting
Being the one left to fill in
For princesses
Who didn't wake from your kiss.

And I get it
Why she kept the apple choked.
Why she bled at the spinning wheel.
Then gave you consent to kiss.

Because you always edge into her happy endings.
For you hold the title of Prince Charming.

Little girls who grow up to be princesses
Are raised to be fragile,
Taught to wait for your kiss.
So they don't discover the strength
Already in their bodies.
Strength enough to escape
The castles with cages
Their daddies built,
Who once upon a time was Prince Charming.

33. Devil Awakened

Shot down.
Torn apart.
Let me bleed
for your gains.

I tried to hold on,
but innocence slipped.

Count your sins
before the doom.

The devil wakes
from abuse.

I was clay.
The one you shaped
Your gift?
An empty vase.

Instead of hope,
you filled me with hate.
Used my trust
to manipulate.

You said
you protected her
from this cruel world.

Now Rapunzel
lies caged, alone,
depressed.

The monster was chained,
blind to the storms
born inside her head.

Ruthless mistakes
aiming to devastate.
But circumstances cut through
a part of her surfaced
she never knew.

You made this weapon
without thinking.
Expecting it
to be selective?

Alas.
I have unleashed.
Oh, the havoc I'll wreak.

You will witness
casualties
of those who are guilty
and also the sinless

34. Games of mind

You play with lives.
Like dice.
Throwing, rolling,
Watching us collide.

Petty.
Wicked.
Mind games.

You feed me fables
Till my eyes go blind.
Tangled in lies
I can't unwind.

Charming tricks
Hidden up your sleeves.
You numb me.
Then deceive.

Do you fear
I'll speak?
To all the victims
Of your sick little mind games?

Maybe you found the one.
A piece of your soul.
Did she change you?
Or remind you
Of every defeat?

The look.
The spark.
Everything I craved...
Given to her.

You fell in love with her.
She turned to stone
The night you lay with me.
Yet... she let you go home.

I was spiralling,
When she won.
I gave everything.
Yet she took the throne.

As I bled to defeat,
She won the game.
Won the war.

35. Lethal Saviour

You curled in drooling poison,
I drank it like my elixir.
You urged me
so I dove in deep,
without any fear.

But you held back,
and you stepped back.
My saviour!
Like a devil concealed
behind the veil of my warrior.

Twisting minds
with your seductive knife,
your infatuation
turned into my curse of life.

I've now turned into a masochist,
entangled in this cruel fantasy.
I am cemented
in this loop of agony.

Because you stabbed hard,
and you ran fast,

My saviour!
now ripped of hope,
Questioning my behavior.

So I call you a sinner.
I will say you are my killer.

I was a glacier;
your love turned me into vapour.
I am a lost letter,
a cracked mirror.

I kissed my beast
and that kiss
turned me into a monster.

36. Friendship Bracelet

Are you still looking for your friendship bracelet?
Remember those beads you picked from different boxes
some of them sparkled.
You hoped to share their glimmer.

Have you realized yet
that they are broken diamonds,
and it is only the dust that glitters?

I still hold the old beads close.
Of course, there are scratches
old fights forgiven and forgotten in time.
They cupped my tears,
a lesson against the flames I might hold again.
They might not have sparkled like those diamonds,
but they weren't scattered away.

Our string is still strong.
Our knot will last lifelong.

Sometimes I suffer from guilt
that new beads found my hand.
They came from a different age,
when taxes and responsibilities grew on you like hair.

But it was good to have some extra beads to spare.

Now I ask you:
walk up to the mirror.
Talk to the image looking back.

That pearl you see
it is the greatest ornament you ever had.

I know, sometimes you feel that oyster who birthed you
she is your best friend.
She did love you unconditionally; there is no doubt in that.
But no one can hold you better than your own hands.

Friendship bracelets last forever
because you are the string that holds them together.
That makes you your greatest friend.

37. New Poem

She came to life.
To fly high.
To be great.

But the wind,
It defied her.
With a mask on its face.

She can't love.
She can't leave.
They control
Even what she believes.

Mannequin with soul.
Mannequin with soul.

Born as a mannequin with a soul.
For their aims.
For their stakes.
A trophy.
On their cabinet.

She watched her dreams
Stripped away.

So they could mould her.
In their ways.

Mannequin with soul.
Mannequin with soul.

Born as a mannequin with a soul.
She chose to live.
Not just survive.

But the truth
It would cost her.
So she chose to lie.

Now the monsters
Snap their claws out.
Wounded,
She's yanked back
To the ground.

Mannequin with soul.
Mannequin with soul.
Born as a mannequin with a soul.

38. Tragic Ending

I dreamt of a rose
in the desert sand,
scorching sun, barren land.
Still, it grew,
with the love we had.
Still, we grew,
hand in hand.

Oh, how hard I fell
you will never understand.

Was it truth, or a lie,
that I drank?
Your words
my weakness, my strength.

I felt alive
when I woke up in your bed,
addicted to your touch,
and the pain you shed.

When the storm came,
I saw you disappear
the promise you broke,

vanishing in the smoke.

With your cigarette burns
still buried in my hand,
you found another
to hold.

You left, bruised;
I lie here, wounded within.

What you stabbed
may never heal.

Is this my tragic ending?
I don't know what to believe.

You left, or were you made to leave?
The question keeps strangling me.

www.ingramcontent.com/pod-product-compliance
Lightning Source LLC
Chambersburg PA
CBHW060204050426
42446CB00013B/2983